First Printing, 2017

ISBN-13: 978-1543236613
ISBN-10: 1543236618

For all the cool colorists across the world who encouraged me to keep on drawing and bringing you yet another book. Thank you so much for your love and encouragement.

And special thanks to my brilliant colorist team, Cindy Nation, Debbie West Cumming, Dee Dee Boseman, Jennifer Owen, Jody Ann Savage, Lori Delgado, Margolet Van Zyl, Marley Morris, Michelle A. Turner, Naomi McClelland Handsaker and Tammy Boykin Lenze.

Special thanks to Michelle A. Turner for this lovely book cover.

IMPORTANT INFORMATION FOR USING THIS BOOK

- This book contains 24 hand-drawn illustrations to color, each is printed SINGLE SIDED (back is blank). 20 winged fairies plus two types of bonus pages of dresses with mannequins!

- The pages are printed on #60 lb bright white paper which performs well for all brands of colored pencils and crayons, without the need of a blotter page.

- To avoid any "Uh Oh's" and the associated disappointment, **Marker and Gel Pen users are STRONGLY ENCOURAGED to USE A BLOTTER SHEET** behind the drawing to avoid any possibility of bleed through to the next page. Several blank blotter and color testing pages are provided at the end of this book.

- Most IMPORTANT of all: Relax, have fun, stand-up and stretch often, and remember that sometimes the most beautiful things come from what we think at first are mistakes, but which turn out to be art's way of working magic!

This Book Belongs To

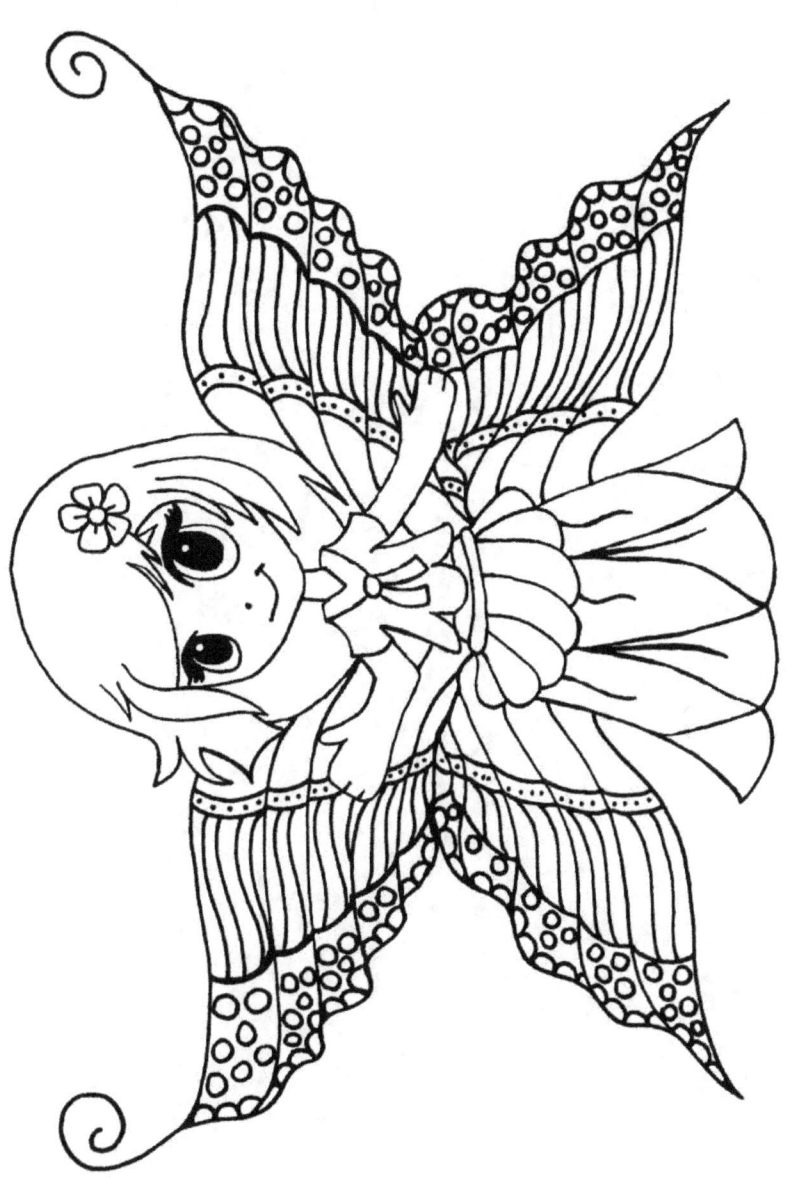

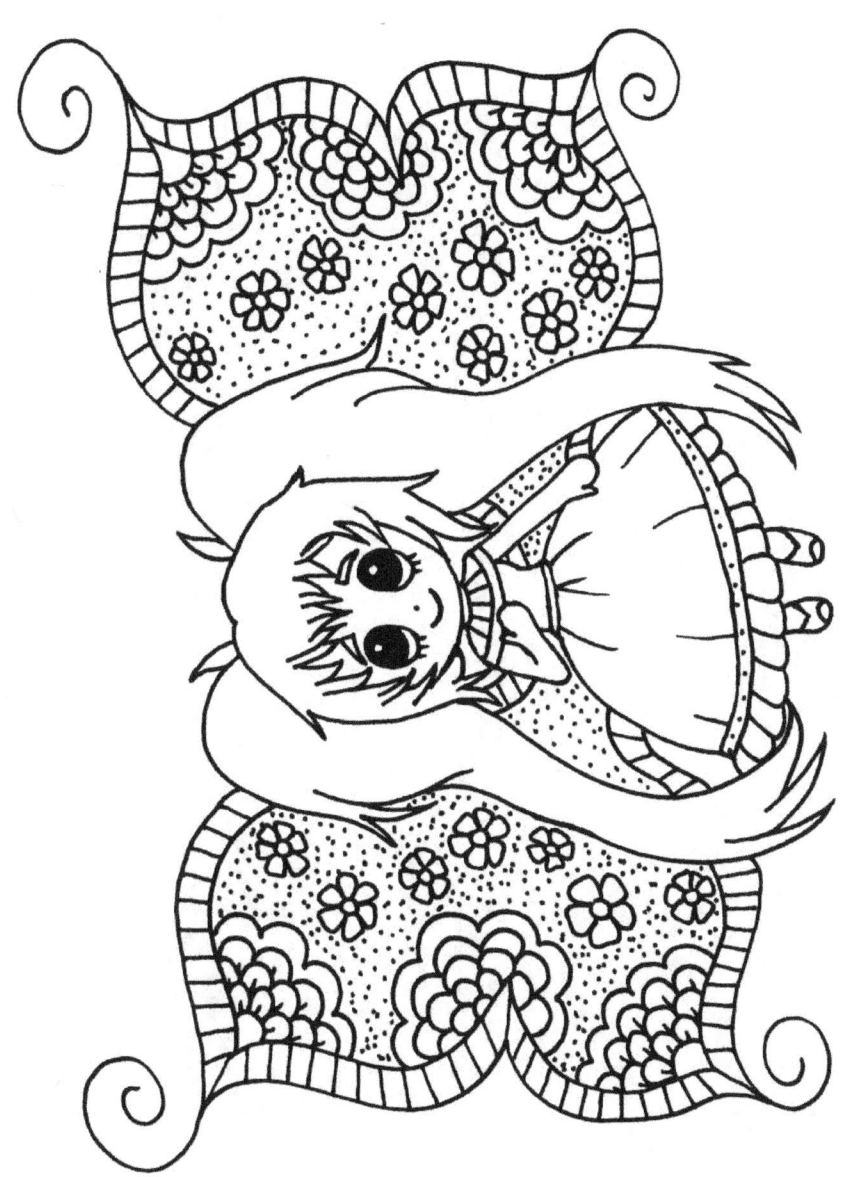

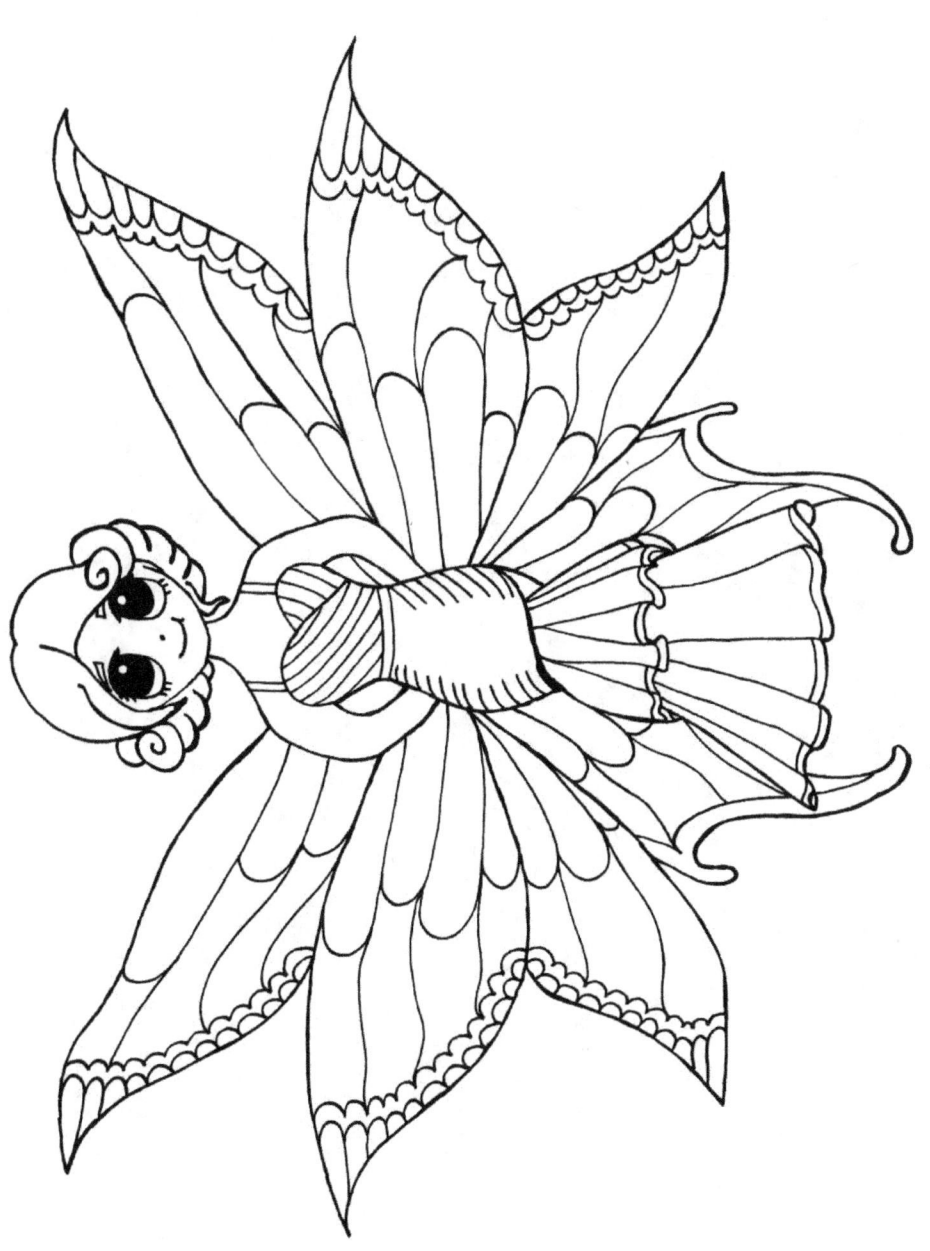

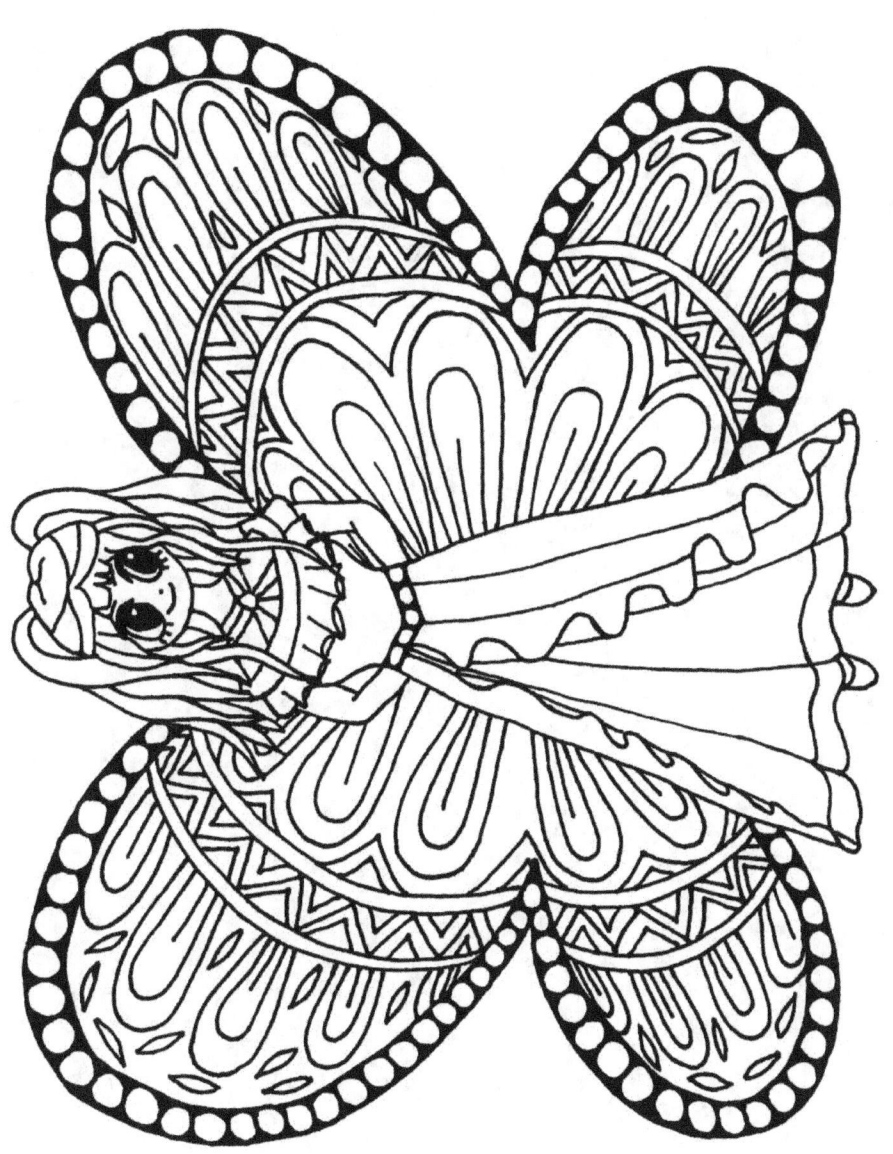

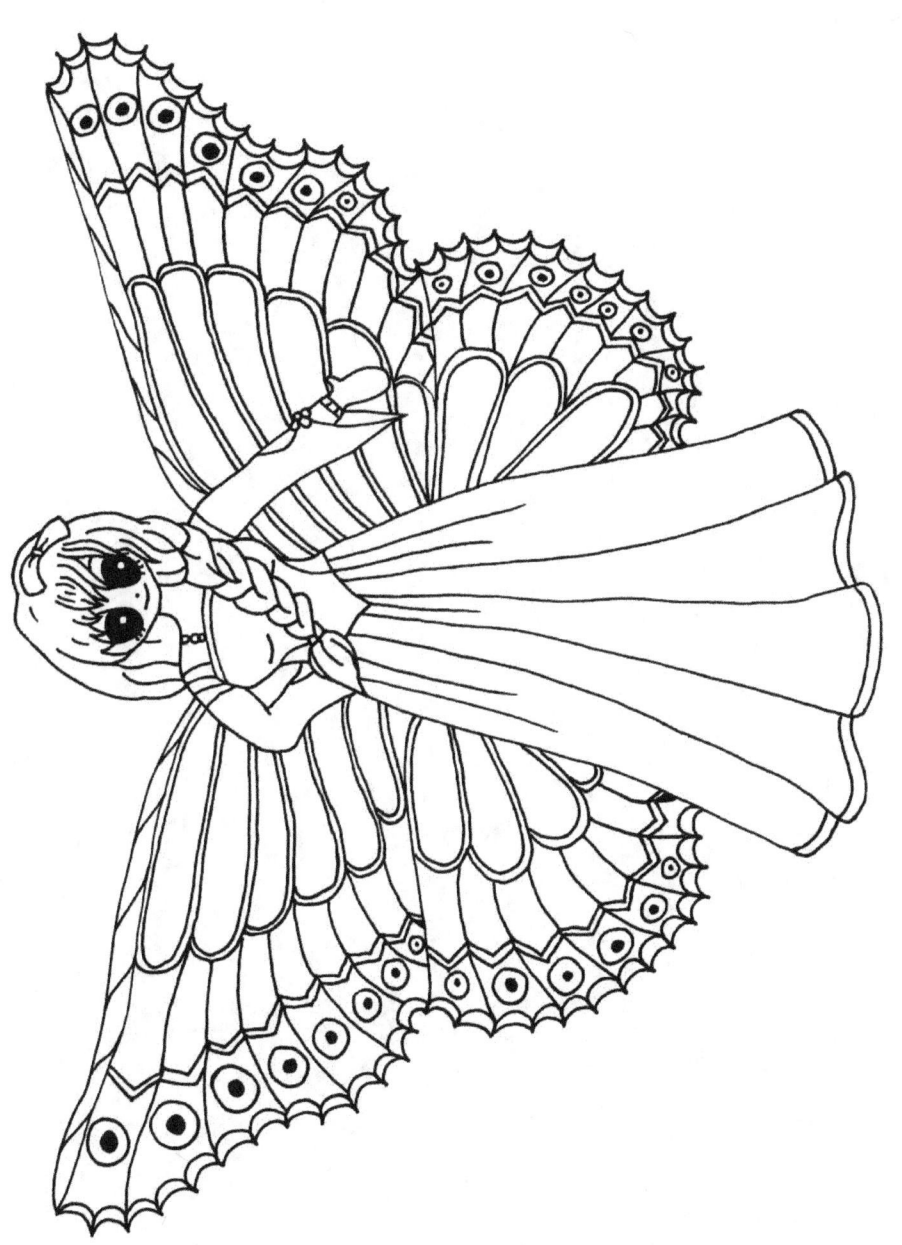

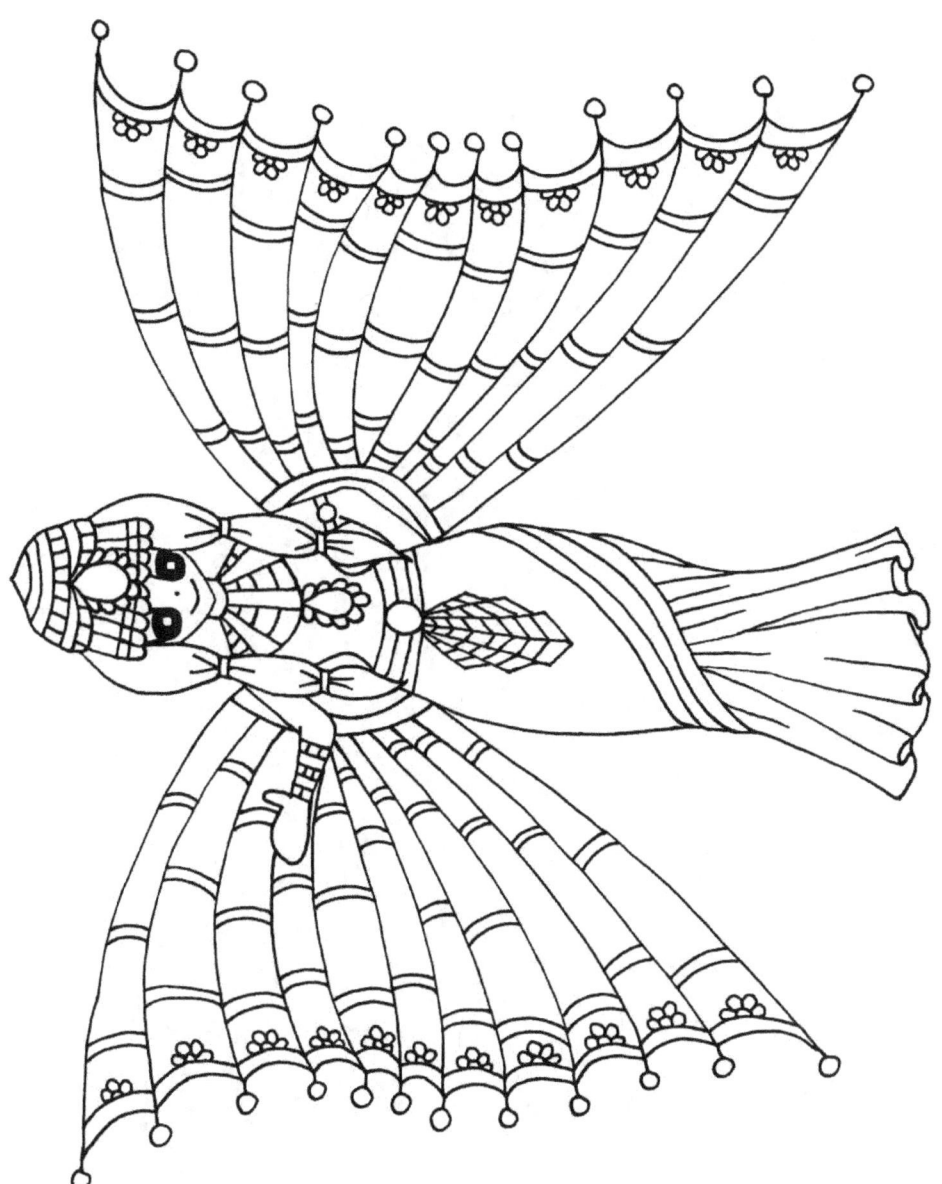

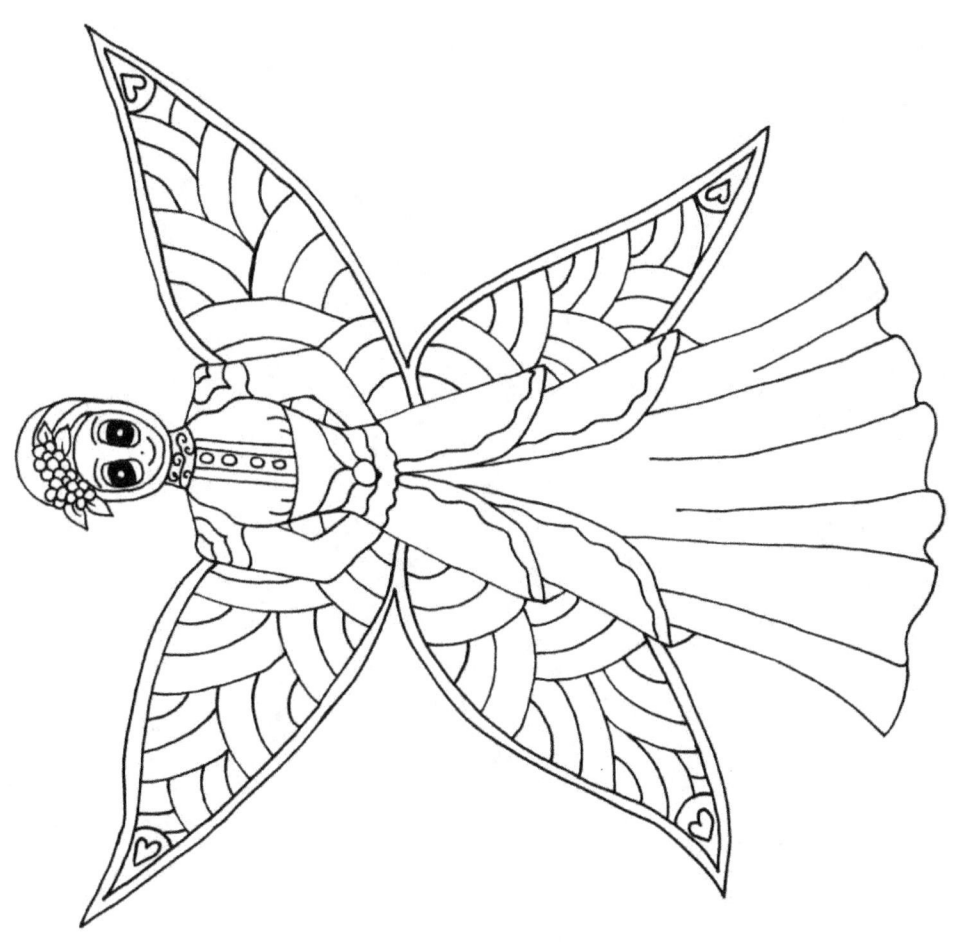

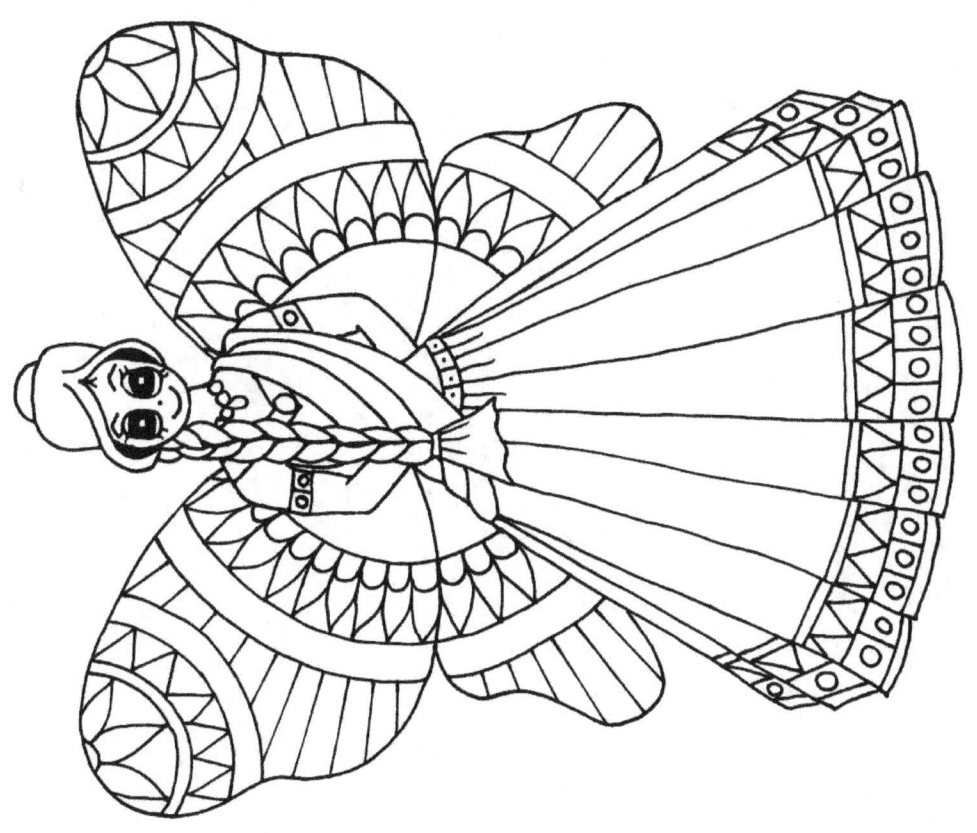

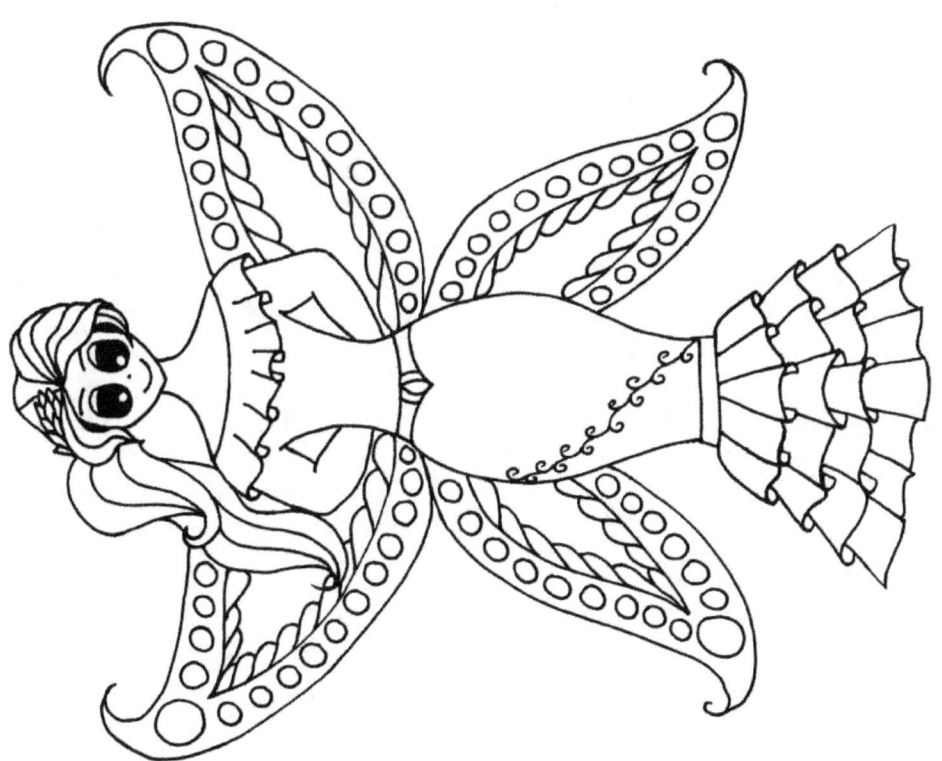

Bonus Pages

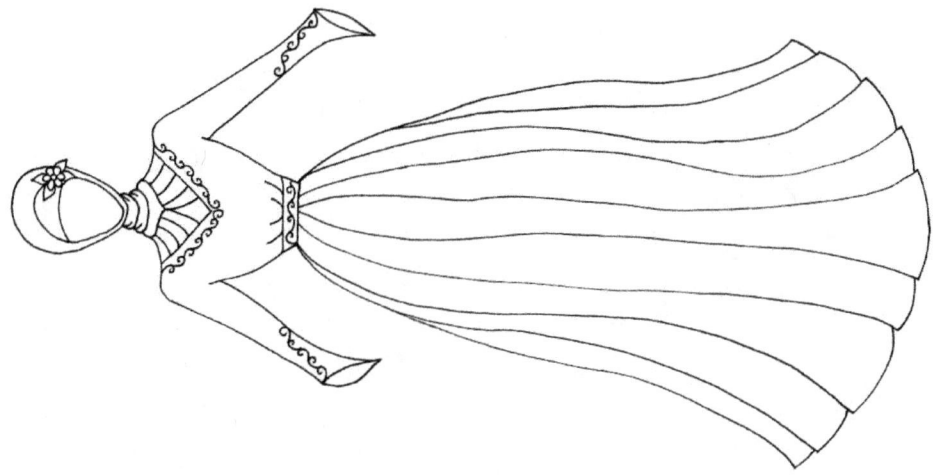

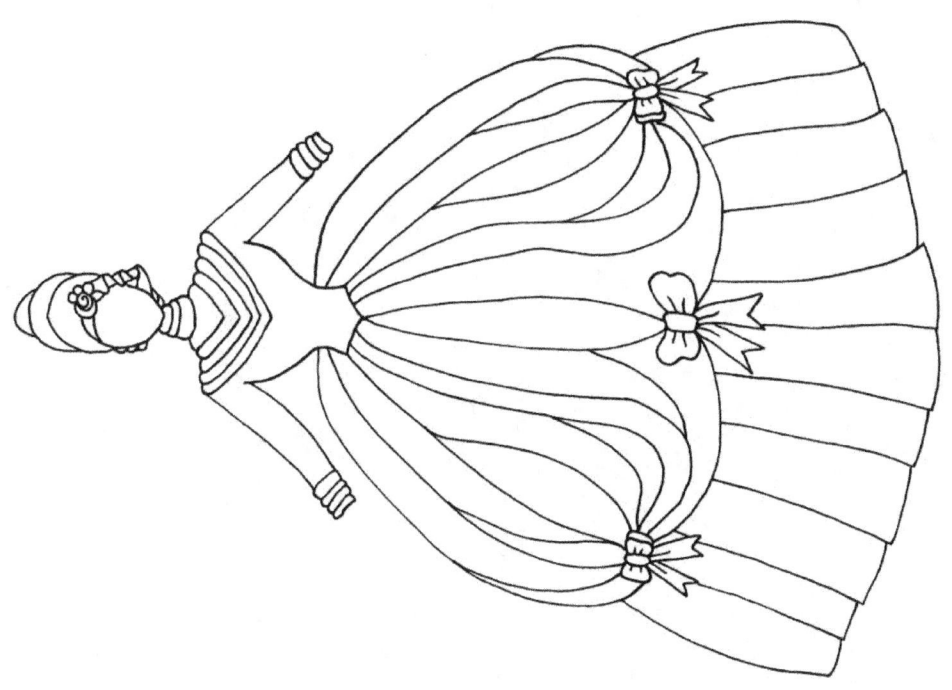

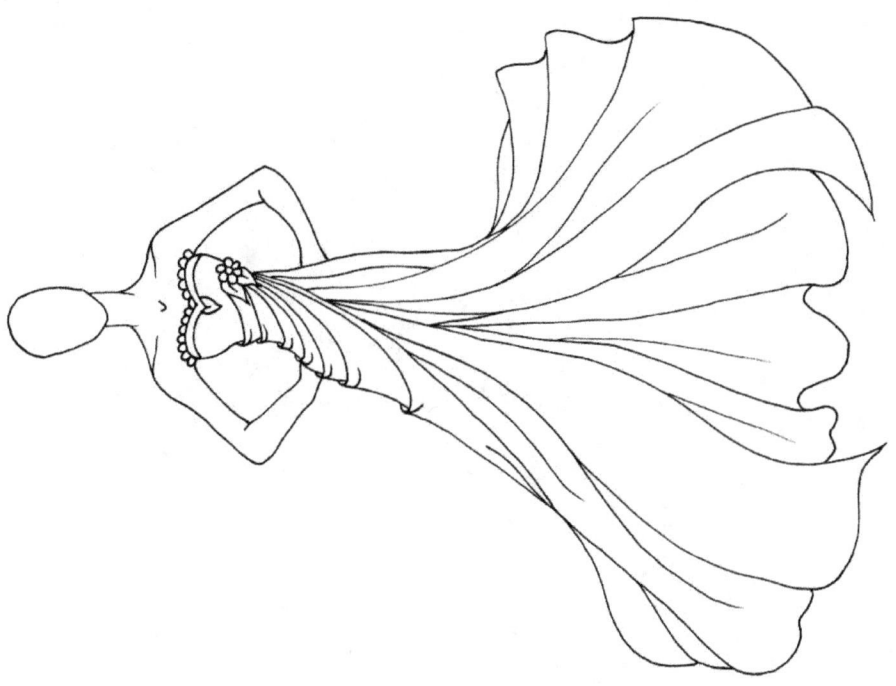

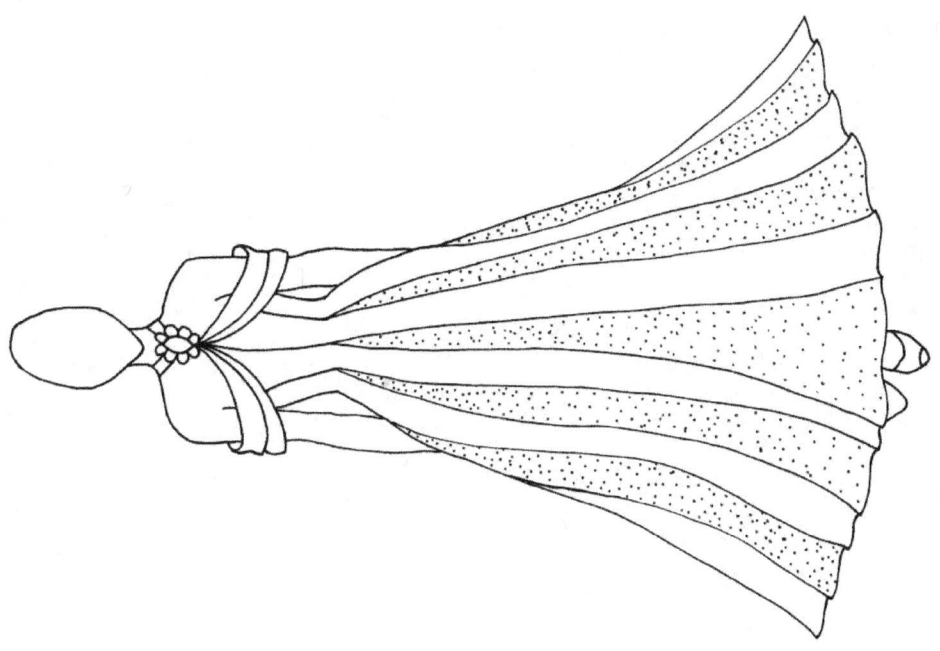

www.ingramcontent.com/pod-product-compliance
Lightning Source LLC
Chambersburg PA
CBHW081418280526

45788CB00009B/3149